favor of crows

NEW AND COLLECTED HAIKU

Gerald Vizenor

Wesleyan University Press   Middletown, Connecticut

WESLEYAN POETRY

Wesleyan University Press
Middletown CT 06459
www.wesleyan.edu/wespress
© 2014, 1999, 1984, 1964, Gerald Vizenor
Manufactured in the United States of America
Designed by Mindy Basinger Hill
Typeset in 11pt Arno Pro
Wesleyan University Press is a member of the Green Press Initiative.
The paper used in this book meets their minimum
requirement for recycled paper.

Library of Congress Cataloging-in-Publication Data

Vizenor, Gerald Robert, 1934–
[Poems. Selections]
Favor of Crows : New and Collected Haiku / Gerald Vizenor.
pages   cm.—(Wesleyan Poetry series)
ISBN 978-0-8195-7432-9 (cloth : alk. paper) —
ISBN 978-0-8195-7433-6 (ebook)
I. Title.
PS3572.I9F39 2014
811'.54 — dc23   2013037645

5   4   3   2   1

*The author and publisher gratefully acknowledge
the illustrations by Robert Houle.*

In Memory of Six Poets and Teachers

Matsuo Bashō, Yosa Buson, Kobayashi Issa

Ezra Pound, Eda Lou Walton, Edward Copeland

♦

The apparition of these faces in the crowd;

Petals on a wet, black bough.

"In a Station of the Metro," Ezra Pound

♦

I would be free of you, my body;

Free of you, too, my little soul.

"Beyond Sorrow," Eda Lou Walton

♦

The first to come

I am called

Among the birds.

I bring the rain

Crow is my name

"Song of the Crows," Henry Selkirk

contents

haiku scenes

AN INTRODUCTION

The heart of haiku is a tease of nature, a concise, intuitive, and original moment. Haiku is visionary, a timely meditation, an ironic manner of creation, and a sense of motion, and, at the same time, a consciousness of seasonal impermanence.

Haiku scenes are tricky fusions of emotion, ethos, and a sense of survivance. The aesthetic creases, or precise, perceptive turns, traces, and cut of words in haiku, are the stray shadows of nature in reverie and memory.

The original moments in haiku scenes are virtual, the fugitive turns and transitions of the seasons, an interior perception of motion, and that continuous sense of presence and protean nature.

Haiku was my first sense of totemic survivance in poetry, the visual and imagistic associations of nature, and of perception and experience. The metaphors in my initial haiku scenes were teases of nature and memory. The traces of my imagistic names cut to the seasons, not to mere imitation, or the cosmopolitan representations and ruminations of an image in a mirror of nature.[1]

PINE ISLANDS

Matsushima, by chance of the military, was my first connection with haiku images and scenes, the actual places the moon rose over those beautiful pine islands in the *haibun*, or prose haiku, of Matsuo Bashō.

"Much praise had already been lavished upon the wonders of the islands of Matsushima," Bashō writes in *The Narrow Road to the Deep North*, translated by Nobuyuki Yuasa. "Yet if further praise is possible, I would like to say that here is the most beautiful spot in the whole country of Japan.... The islands are situated in a bay about three miles wide in every direction and open to the sea.... Islands are piled above islands, and islands are joined to islands, so that they look exactly like parents caressing their children or walking with them arm in arm. The pines are of the freshest green, and their branches are curved in exquisite lines, bent by the wind constantly blowing through them."[2]

Matsushima and the pine islands are forever in my memories and in the book. I was there, in that same *haibun* sense of presence and place, almost three centuries later in the motion of the seasons, and tried my best to envision the actual presence of Bashō at Matsushima.

water striders
master bashō wades near shore
out of reach

The United States Army, by chance, sent me to serve first in a tank battalion on Hokkaido and later at a military post near Sendai in northern Japan. I was eighteen years old at the time. Haiku, in a sense, inspired me on the road as a soldier in another culture and gently turned me back to the seasons, back to the traces of nature and the tease of native reason and memories. The imagistic scenes of haiku were neither exotic nor obscure to me. Nature then and now was a sense of presence, changeable and chancy, not some courtly tenure of experience, or pretense of comparative and taxonomic discovery.

Haiku scenes are similar, in a sense, to the original dream songs and visionary images of the *anishinaabe,* the Chippewa or Ojibwe, on the White Earth Reservation in Minnesota. I was inspired by these imagistic literary connections at the time. The associations seem so natural to me now. Once, words and worlds apart in time and place, these poetic images of haiku and dream songs came together more by chance than fate, and later by intuition and consideration.

Many *anishinaabe* dream songs are about the presence of animals, birds, and other totemic creatures in experience, visions, and in memory. The same can be said about haiku scenes, that the visions of nature are the perceptions and traces of memory.

Yosa Buson wrote haiku scenes that suggested a longing for

home. These poems are so "poignant that he has come to be known as 'the poet of nostalgia' in recent decades," wrote Makoto Ueda in *The Path of Flowering Thorn*. Buson, who was born some seventy years after Matsuo Bashō, traveled to the pine islands and wrote at least one poem about Matsushima.

in matsushima
a man gazing at the moon
empty seashells

There, at Matsushima, "Bashō was so overwhelmed by the moonlit scenery that he was not able to compose" observed Ueda. "The moon view in Buson's hokku may well be Bashō, who became 'empty' like a pair of seashells on the shore and could not write. Or the man may represent all visitors to Matsushima, Buson himself included, who are too dazzled by its scenic beauty to find words to express it. And those speechless admirers are numberless like seashells on the shore of Matsushima."[3]

The poetic forms of *waka, tanka, haikai no renga, hokku,* and *haiku* are interrelated by artistic entitlement, manner, means, and practice in the literary history of Japan. Waka, for instance, a classical form of poetry, is related to tanka, a five-line poem of thirty-one sounds or syllables. The first and third lines are five syllables, and the second, fourth, and fifth lines are each seven syllables. Tanka poems were included in the *Kojiki,* the oldest collection of literary narratives, and in the great *Man'yōshū,* the oldest collection of poetry. These two anthologies were compiled in the eighth century in Japan.

Haikai no renga is the customary style of linked seventeen syllable poems. Hokku is the name of the first poem or scene in the series, and later the distinction became a haiku scene.

Renga or the creation of linked images was a significant literary practice in the early literature of Japan.

"Renga is important because it is the origin of haiku, and because it continued to be composed for the next eight hundred years, side by side with the later haiku. Bashō, Buson, and Issa were teachers of renga; it was their art and their livelihood," R. H. Blyth pointed out in *A History of Haiku*. "Haiku have no rhyme, little rhythm, assonance, alliteration, or intonation," and in haiku, "two different things that are joined in sameness are poetry and sensation, spirit and matter. . . . The coldness of a cold day, the heat of a hot day, the smoothness of a stone, the whiteness of a seagull, the distance of the far-off mountains, the smallness of a small flower, the dampness of the rainy season, the quivering of the hairs of a caterpillar in the breeze—these things, without any thought or emotion or beauty or desire are haiku."[4]

HAIKU MOMENT

"The essence of all nature poetry is animism," observed Blyth. "Haiku is an ascetic art, an artistic asceticism. Of the two elements, the ascetic is more rare, more difficult, of more value than the artistic."[5] Likewise, *anishinaabe* animism, that sense of natural presence, totemic association, and imagistic moments in a dream song, is an artistic union of nature, intuition, and emotion, or natural reason of the seasons and native survivance.

Kenneth Yasuda writes in *The Japanese Haiku* that haiku is an aesthetic experience, and the sense of a *"haiku moment"* is eternal. "Every word, then, in a haiku, rather than *contributing* to the meaning as words do in a novel or sonnet, *is* an experience." That moment is natural reason in a haiku scene. "A haiku moment is a kind of aesthetic moment—a moment in which the words which created the experience and the experience itself can become one."[6]

Haiku scenes and *anishinaabe* dream songs are moments of creation, and, in that sense, the actual experiences of nature are survivance. The *anishinaabe* dream songs are imagistic visions of motion and, at the same time, a personal tease of nature. Haiku scenes and dream songs are created by natural reason, a sense of presence, and not by aesthetic theories.

Many haiku scenes, even in translation, aroused in me a sense of natural presence. That intuitive moment, a *haiku moment,* is natural reason: the image of leaves floating silently beneath a waterfall, sunrise on the wings of a dragonfly, the slow march of a blue heron in the shallows, the great shadows of sandpipers on the beach, cracks of thunder in the ice, tiny blue flowers in a vein of granite, the return of the juncos to the bare birch trees, and the favor of crows. These are scenes of motion, the totemic traces and unities of natural reason and survivance.

Haiku scenes are accessible in nature and culture, the subject and object of perception and experience, and that alone was more than any poetry had ever given me in the past. Haiku from the start turned my thoughts to chance, ephemerality, and impermanence, the very traces of a creative tease and presence in nature.

WORLD OF DEW

"I knew well it was no use to cry, that water once flown past the bridge does not return, and blossoms that are scattered are gone beyond recall," Kobayashi Issa writes about the death of his daughter in *The Year of My Life.* "Yet try as I would, I could not, simply could not cut the binding cord of human love."[7] Sato, his daughter, is remembered in this poignant haiku scene translated by Nobuyuki Yuasa:

> the world of dew
> is the world of dew
> and yet . . .
> and yet . . .

Stephen Addiss observed in *The Art of Haiku* that *tsuyu no yo wa,* "this world of dew," is the "most quoted of all Issa haiku." The poem was written after his infant daughter Sato died. "It perfectly captures the moment when sincere religious understanding meets the deepest feelings of the heart."[8]

I first read haiku as evocative memories of the motion of seasons, and yet the scenes, the perceptive, emotive moments, connections, and associations, were ironic traces of my own transience and impermanence in nature. Haiku created a sense of presence, and, at the same time, reminded me of a nature that was already wounded, desecrated, removed, and an absence in many places on the earth. Nature is a presence not a permanence, and a *haiku moment* is a sense of presence, a perceptive moment of survivance.

My very first literary creations were haiku scenes, and since then, that imagistic sense of nature has always been present in my writing. I may never know if my haiku are right by nature, only that the scenes are my best memories. In this way, my sense of presence, haiku creations, and survivance is in nature and in the book.

Yosa Buson, the son of a farmer, was born more than two centuries ago, and yet we met by chance and by nature in the to nature in an *anishinaabe* dream song. The poet singer listens to the turnout of the seasons, and then puts the words of his song directly to the wind and sky. The gesture, in part, is ironic, a delightful native tease of nature.

"With a large bird above me, I am walking in the sky," is the translation of another avian vision by an *anishinaabe* poet singer who was heard more than a century ago in northern Minnesota.

Frances Densmore, the honorable recorder of native songs and ceremonies, translated these *anishinaabe* dream songs at the turn of the twentieth century. "Many of the songs are taught only to those who pay for the privilege of learning them, and all the songs are recorded in mnemonics on strips of birch bark. This record serves as a reminder of the essential idea of the song and is different in its nature from our system of printing. The Indian picture preserves the idea of the song, while our printed page preserves the words which are supposed to express the idea but which often express it very imperfectly," observed Densmore.[14] The songs are creative, reverie, perceptive moments, similar to the traces of nature in haiku scenes.

as my eyes
look across the prairie
I feel the summer
in the spring

overhanging clouds
echoing my words
with a pleasing sound

across the earth
everywhere
making my voice heard[15]

The *anishinaabe* "ability to dream was cultivated from earliest childhood," writes Densmore in *Chippewa Customs*. Dreams were a source of wisdom, and children were encouraged to remember the stories of their dreams. "Thus the imagination was stimulated, and there arose a keen desire to see something extraordinary in sleep." The *anishinaabe* "say that in their dreams they often returned to the previous state of existence." Some dreams had such great power "that a man had been known to assume the form which had been his in a previous existence, and which had formed the subject of his dream." The stories of great dreams secured a sense of "protection, guidance, and assistance."[16] Clearly, the perceptive moments of native dreams, in the sense of the *anishinaabe*, were stories of natural reason and survivance, not possessive, reductive, or a passive absence. Native dreams were visionary and created an active sense of presence.

My introduction to haiku, by chance of the military, made it easier to understand natural reason and the survivance of native dream songs and literature. How ironic that my service as a soldier would lead to a literary association of haiku, and an overture to *anishinaabe* dream songs. Truly, haiku enhanced my perception and experience of dream songs, and my consideration of native reason, comparative philosophies, and survivance.

CULTURAL STRATEGIES

"On the one hand there is the disposition of things—their condition, configuration, and structure. On the other there is force and movement," François Jullien observed in *The Propensity of Things*. "The static versus the dynamic. But this dichotomy, like all dichotomies, is abstract. It is a temporary means for the mind to represent reality, one that simplifies as it illuminates."

What, then, really exists, "stranded between these two terms of the dichotomy," the static and dynamic? "How can we conceive of the dynamic in terms of the static, in terms of 'disposition'?"

The Chinese concept of *shi* is a critical disposition of dynamic literature, and the efficacy of philosophy. Jullien wrote that Liu Xie, a sixth-century literary philosopher, "offers us a fine image for the dynamism at work in a literary text: when one sets down the brush at the end of a paragraph, it is like feathering an oar while rowing. The boat continues to drift forward just as, at the completion of a passage, the text continues to progress. A 'surplus of *shi*' carries it forward, leading to the point where it will link up with its own continuation. A text exists not only through its 'order' and 'coherence,' but also through its 'flow' and unfolding.'"

The imagistic scenes flow by the cultural strategies of tone and dynamic rhythms, and by an interior sense of natural reason. Many haiku scenes have *shi,* and the disposition, the temperament, inclination, the mood and aesthetic tendencies, or intuitive moments, continue to move in nature and in our memories, and in the book.

Jullien noted in his introduction that the "term *shi* is the same as the word *yi,* which is believed to represent a hand holding something, a symbol of power." Xu Shen, the second-century lexicographer, "thinks that what is held in the hand is a clod of earth." The diacritic radical *li,* or force, was added to the character later.[17]

"Aesthetics plays an exceedingly important role in Chinese writing, more so than in any other system of writing. Calligraphy has been elevated to an art form," wrote John DeFrancis in *The Chinese Language*. Xu Shen compiled an etymological dictionary of more than nine thousand characters in some five hundred "semantic keys," or "significs." The significs are otherwise named "radicals," or the basic, significant, semantic elements of characters. "Most striking of all is the fact that the Chinese chose a semantic basis rather than a phonetic one for their system of classification."[18]

Jullien considered *shi* a "touchtone" character, and, as an imprecise word, *shi* is semantic and more than a concept; *shi* is a poetic disposition and "intuition of efficacy."

The poem "must be conceived all at once, from start to finish, as a continuous *variation*," wrote Jullien. "In poetry, as in every thing else, dynamism must be renewed, through internal contrasts and shifts from one pole to the other, in order to be continuous." The "poetic *shi*," or the "*dispositional propensity* born of that emotion," becomes the visionary transmotion of the expression and a creative moment.

Jullien wrote that a poem is "a single surge of internal energy," and quotes Wang Fuzhi that a poem is "not like 'a melon,' which can be 'divided into slices.'" Rather, the "continuity is intrinsic."[19]

Kitaro Nishida, the Japanese philosopher of experience and reality, wrote in *An Inquiry into the Good,* "What people usually refer to as *nature* is what remains after the subjective aspect, the unifying activity, is removed from concrete reality. For this reason, there is no self in nature," and, he observed, "that it is not that experience exists because there is an individual, but that an individual exists because there is experience. I thus arrived at the idea that experience is more fundamental than individual differences, and in this way I was able to avoid solipsism." By solipsism, he means "the theory that the self can know only its own experience," or the idea that the self is the only source of reality.[20]

Any hint of the self is absent in most haiku scenes, but even when subjective experience is mentioned it is not solipsistic or the self of nature. Issa, for instance, is moved by nature, and includes references to his presence in haiku scenes. "Issa's whole life was a tragedy," Blyth wrote in *Haiku: Eastern Culture*. "He was one of those men who attract failure and misfortune." Issa was moved by a sense of fate. "Life goes along joyfully and painfully, with ecstasy and anguish, and Issa goes with it. He does not praise or condemn."[21]

for you fleas too
the night must be long
it must be lonely

"Issa's sympathies were always with small and weak animals, perhaps because he identified himself with them, as the victim of his stepmother's cruelty," and other burdens, Donald Keene wrote in *World Within Walls*.[22]

skinny frog
don't be discouraged
issa is here

Issa must be here too, a sense of presence in the constant cut of words, transmotion of translation, and, of course, in the creative consideration of readers. I first read his haiku two centuries after he cajoled that skinny frog and then created this scene at Lake Itasca, Minnesota.

tricky frogs
croak a haiku in the marsh
skinny issa[23]

Likewise, the *anishinaabe* created an elusive sense of self and presence in their dream songs, but not *the* self of nature. "The sky loves to hear me sing," and, "with a large bird, I am walking in the sky," and "overhanging clouds echoing my words with a pleasing sound," and "the wind carries me across the sky," and "my feathers sailing on the breeze," and "I will prove alone the power of my spirit," are the imagistic and ironic scenes of visionaries, the motion of intuition, and transformation of the self, not merely the subjective, solipsistic estates of a material nature.

the first to come
epithet among the birds
bringing the rain
crow is my name

This *anishinaabe* dream song is about the arrival of spring and the crows, a natural transmotion of the seasons. The singer has taken the name of the crow, the favor of the crow, and teases a shamanic, visionary voice of nature. The crow, or *aandeg*, is a sign of wisdom, maybe even a trace of tragic wisdom.

overhanging clouds
echoing my words
with a pleasing sound
across the earth
everywhere
making my voice heard[24]

Shamanic visions come to light in a summer storm. Frances Densmore noted that the singer "hears the reverberations of the thunder and in his dream or trance he composes a song concerning it." Again, the scene is created in nature, the visionary sound of the storm, but is not a subjective voice of nature. The *anishinaabe* do not have a word for the concept of nature. The native traces and tease of the seasons are distinct, direct, and visionary.

from the half
of the sky
that which lives there
is coming
and makes a noise

Densmore observed that the singer of this dream song imagines that the thunder *manidoo,* or spirit, "sometimes makes a voice to warn him of its approach." The voice *is* the *manidoo,* not a mere representation of the native spirit. "The idea which underlies the song is, that which lives in the sky is coming and, being friendly, it makes a noise to let me know of its approach."[25] The *anishinaabe* word for thunder is *biidwewidam,* and means to "come making noise." The voice of thunder is in motion, a dynamic sound, not subjective, or passive mimicry.

The self, or personal voice, in haiku scenes and *anishinaabe* dream songs are dynamic and visionary; appropriately the dispositions of *manidoo* and *shi* are perceptive moments of presence in nature, but not the subjective voices of nature. The creation of a scene in a dream song, and the perceptive moment of a haiku scene are carried into nature. The voice, tone, and brevity of inspired words continue as cultural strategies in the natural motion of images, in the tease and discussion of transience in nature, and a sense of presence in the book.

"Only when there is a unifying self does nature have a goal, take on significance, and become a truly living nature," wrote Kitaro Nishida. "The unifying power that is the life of such nature is not an abstract concept artificially created by our thought but a fact that appears in our intuition." He pointed out, that artists are "people who most excel in this kind of intuition."[26] The intuitive moments and meditation of haiku scenes create the experiences, memories, and survivance of nature.

Suzuki wrote in *Zen and Japanese Culture* that haiku "like Zen, abhors egoism in any form of assertion. The product of art must be entirely devoid of artifice or ulterior motive of any kind. There ought not to be any presence of a mediatory agent between the artistic inspiration and the mind into which it has come. The author is to be an altogether passive instrument for giving an expression to the inspiration."[27]

The visionary scenes in haiku and native dream songs are intuitive, a dynamic presence that only appear to be passive because it is not the ego or self that discovers and possesses nature in poetry. The voices of thunder and the favor of crows are intuitive, neither passive nor possessive. Suzuki abhors egoism, but the visionary pronouns of nature are intuitive, not a ruse of devotion or the tricky asceticism of Zen Buddhism as often depicted.

Philosophy, religion, and literature are inseparable in many cultures. Characteristically, haiku and *anishinaabe* dream songs are more intuitive than demonstrative; more shadows, suggestions, and concise images than the metes and bounds of linguistic theory and abstract literature.

"The thought process underlying this nondemonstrative approach does not simply rely on language but rather denies it," observed Masao Abe in the introduction to *An Inquiry into the Good* by Nishida. "This separation from language and rational thought is typically found in Zen, which conveys its basic standpoint with the statement, 'No reliance on words or letters; a special transmission apart from doctrinal teaching.' The same attitude appears in Confucius, who proclaims, 'Clever talk and pretentious manner are seldom found in the Good.' We encounter it in ink drawings that negate form and color, Noh theater with its negation of direct or external expression, and Japanese *waka* and *haiku* poetry."

Abe declared that to "generate a creative synthesis of Eastern and Western philosophy, one must include but go beyond the demonstrative thinking that is characteristic of the West." The outcome is an "unobjectifiable ultimate reality," and surely that would become an eternal tease of nature, and a trace of marvelous names. The perceptive moments are haiku scenes, native dreams, and the visionary.

"Thinking and intuition are usually considered to be totally different activities, but when we view them as facts of consciousness we realize that they are the same kind of activity," argued Nishida. "At the base of thinking there is always a certain unifying reality that we can know only through intuition."[28]

HAIKU SCENES

Haiku scenes ascribe the seasons with the stray shadows of words, sunlight on the wings of butterflies, the wind that turns a leaf, a cardinal in the sumac, mounds of snow at twilight. Shadow words are intuitive, concise, the natural motion of memories, and the turn of seasons. Blyth wrote, "Haiku is the result of the wish, the effort, not to speak, not to write poetry, not to obscure further the truth and suchness of a thing with words, with thoughts and feelings." And yet, we read and write with pleasure in the motion of nature and creative literature. Blyth asserted that a "haiku is not a poem, it is not literature; it is a hand beckoning, a door half-opened, a mirror wiped clean. It is a way of returning to nature, to our moon nature, our cherry blossom nature, our falling leaf nature, in short, to our Buddha nature."[29]

Addiss pointed out that "Zen masters did not tend to write haiku very frequently until the modern era, but some monks added haiku inscriptions to their paintings." Zen Buddhism and the principles of austere meditation and transcendence of rationalism influenced Bashō. The sway of his haiku "comes when there is no overt religious reference, but the haiku resonates with Zen spirit. Bashō himself commented that haiku 'is simply what is happening here and now.'" Zen spirit is "presented through his ability to take the ordinary world and perceive unexpected images and interactions."[30]

Matsuo Bashō was born in 1644 at Ueno, near Kyoto. He was troubled, ridden by doubts as a youth, and later turned to Taoism and Zen Buddhism, wrote Makoto Ueda in *Bashō and His Interpreters*. Bashō decided on "*fuga,* an artist's way of life, a reclusive life devoted to a quest for eternal truth in nature." He pursued *fuga* with sincerity; nonetheless, "he had lingering misgivings about its redemptive power. To his last days, he did not seem able to merge poetry with belief completely."[31]

Haruo Shirane pointed out in *Traces of Dreams* that "Bashō initially went to Edo in order to become a haikai master, a marker who could charge fees for grading haikai." However, he soon turned his back "on the most lucrative aspect of haikai. Even as a marker in Edo, Bashō apparently was reluctant to charge fees. Most of his disciples also avoided the profession of a marker." The name of a marker, or grader, was the same as a haikai master. The haikai, from *haikai no renga*, was a comic, communal, linked verse.

"Bashō divides haikai poets into three types," wrote Shirane. The ideal poet is "devoted to the spirit of poetry rather than to the material benefits and who seek the poetic tradition of Teika and Tu Fu." Fujiwara Teika practiced an "allusive variation" of classical literature at the turn of the thirteenth century. Tu Fu, the eighth century Chinese poet, was praised for the density of his images, the fusion of emotions and allusions to culture. Poets of the second type are those with wealth and status who see haikai as a game. The lowest are the poets who garner points. They are "the lost children of poetry," Bashō wrote to a disciple, "and yet they fill the bellies of the marker's wife and children and bring a profit to the landlord, and as a consequence, they are probably better than those who commit serious crimes."[32]

Bashō died on November 28, 1694. He "dictated this hokku to his student Donshu" three days before his death:

> on a journey, ailing
> my dreams roam about
> on a withered moor

"As it was a balmy day, many flies had gathered around the sliding screens, and the students were trying to catch them with a lime stick," wrote Ueda. "Bashō, amused that some were more skillful than others in handling the stick, laughed and said, 'Those flies seem delighted to have a sick man around unexpectedly.' He spoke no more. He breathed his last at around four that afternoon."[33]

Bashō was amused, and that image of the flies moves with me by imagination, experience, and by haiku scenes in the book. Bashō might have teased me over this scene, my haiku about the presence of fat green flies at a restaurant in Ellsworth, Wisconsin:

fat green flies
square dance on the grapefruit
honor your partner[34]

Japanese poets were once the warriors of literary fusions, classical allusions, loyalties, and, of course, created scenes with a sense of chance and impermanence. Many were actual poets of the road, a meditative, situational tradition of literature. Bashō traveled and wrote *haibun,* a distinctive form of prose and haiku, on his journeys to northern Japan.

Haruo Shirane observed that the "*Narrow Road to the Interior* is marked by a great variety of prose styles, which range from a heavily Chinese style to the soft classical style to vernacular prose to a mixture or fusion of all three. In some sections, the style is extremely dense and terse, falling into strict couplets, and in others it resembles the mellifluous, lengthy flow of *The Tale of Genji*." The Matsushima section, for instance, is "extremely Chinese in style and content."

Matsushima, the envisioned presence of the great poet, and the *haibun* scenes he wrote there were extraordinary and memorable three centuries later in my imagination. Naturally, the haibun and haiku moments, poetic images, and the actual presence of the magical pine islands, were a source of inspiration. Bashō was a master of natural reason, the motion of the seasons, and he had put his "body to the wind." I had no idea at the time that the creation of a *haibun* place was a fusion of haiku scenes and literary styles.

"Although often praised as a work of confessional literature or regarded as part of the long tradition of travel accounts, *Narrow Road to the Interior* is best seen as a kind of fiction, loosely based on the actual journey, leaving out most of what actually happened. Key individuals are not mentioned or appear under fictitious or altered names. Bashō added incidents and characters for dramatic effect, and often rearranged or reconstructed those events that did occur. "Bashō depicted an ideal poetic world," wrote Shirane. "Like a linked verse sequence, to which it has often been compared, *Narrow Road to the Interior* has no absolute center, no single overarching perspective. Instead, a focal point emerges, climaxes and then is replaced by a new focal point." These literary fusions are similar to the dreams songs and trail stories of the *anishinaabe* and the fur trade in the Boundary Waters of Minnesota and Ontario.

Europeans have celebrated a travel literature of conquest and exotic discovery. Not only the discovery of "new" worlds, but of new ideas and literary experiences. "But for medieval *waka* and *renga* poets," noted Shirane, "the object of travel was to confirm what already existed, to reinforce the roots of cultural memory."[35] That too was the sentiment of the *anishinaabe*, the native existential sense of travel, totemic associations, and a visionary cultural memory.

Issa wrote *haibun* on his journey, *The Year of My Life*. "At long last I made up my mind to travel north," he wrote in a translation by Nobuyuki Yuasa, "to get more experience in writing *haiku*. No sooner had I slung my beggar's bag round my neck and flung my little bundle over my shoulder than I noticed, to my great surprise, that my shadow was the very image of Saigyo, the famous poet-priest of times gone by." Saigyo was a twelfth-century waka poet and priest.

Issa, at age fifty-seven, writes at the end of *The Year of My Life,* in December 1819, "Those who insist on salvation by faith and devote their minds to nothing else, are bound all the more firmly by their singlemindedness, and fall into the hell of attachment to their own salvation. Again, those who are passive and stand to one side waiting to be saved, consider that they are already perfect and rely rather on Buddha than on themselves to purify their hearts—these, too, have failed to find the secret of genuine salvation. The question then remains—how do we find it? But the answer, fortunately, is not difficult.

"We should do far better to put this vexing problem of salvation out of our minds altogether and place our reliance neither on faith nor on personal virtue, but surrender ourselves completely to the will of Buddha. Let him do as he will with us—be it to carry us to heaven, or to hell. Herein lies the secret."[36] The motion of twilight, transitory seasons, chance, irony, stray shadows, and rumors of a sense of presence are common sentiments of experience in haiku and *anishinaabe* dream songs, stories, and contemporary literature.

Issa, the "poet of destiny," died eight years later. The frogs continue to croak his name, skinny Issa in the secret marsh, and he is celebrated everywhere by crickets, mosquitoes, flies, many insects, and many birds in the voices of nature and survivance.

Robert Aitken pointed out in *A Zen Wave* that any "distinct form of art implies a characteristic vision of completeness, and the completeness of the haiku form, as Bashō perfected it, is not just a matter of brevity and the emphatic arrangement of seventeen syllables. One Western reader said that going through a collection of haiku was like being pecked to death by doves."

Clearly that reader was preoccupied with the intransigent converse of a haiku scene, and failed to notice the precise moment of chance and liberty in a haiku image, and a sense of presence and survivance, not salvation or death by nature.

Aitken proposed, however, that the disappointment of the unnamed reader "with the haiku collection would not have been allayed by an understanding of that convention. I would guess that it arises from precisely what Bashō himself wanted the form, each instance of it, to be. Not static, as the unsympathetic Western reader might suppose. But dynamic in the manner of a single frame of thought—an instant that is unique, indivisible, and therefore whole."[37]

The motion of the seasons portrayed in haiku scenes is a tease of nature; the imagistic tease of constant natural motion, the bounce, wither, and impermanence of cherry blossoms in the snow, the shiver of the autumn moon on the river, moths in a paper lantern, and the rebound of crows in a sudden storm. These haiku scenes nurture a sense of presence, survivance, and visionary memory.

The *Favor of Crows* is a collection of my original haiku scenes, new, selected, and revised from seven of my haiku books published in the past fifty years. My very first book of haiku was a collection of fifty-six scenes, fourteen in each of four seasons, privately printed in a limited edition at the Minnesota State Reformatory in Saint Cloud. I was a recent college graduate and served as a corrections agent or social worker at the time and paid inmates in the print shop to print and saddle stitch a hundred copies of *Two Wings the Butterfly* in 1962.[38] My second book of haiku scenes, *Raising the Moon Vines,* was published two years later by Callimachus Publishing Company, and reprinted in 1968 and 1999 by Norton Stillman, owner of the Nodin Press in Minneapolis.[39]

Seventeen Chirps was published in 1964, a limited hardcover edition printed on laid finish paper and hand bound by the Lund Bindery in Minneapolis.⁴⁰ The Nodin Press published *Slight Abrasions: A Dialogue in Haiku* by Gerald Vizenor and Jerome Downs in 1966.⁴¹ My fifth book of haiku, *Empty Swings,* was published in 1967.⁴² *Matsushima: Pine Islands,* the first collection of my original haiku scenes, was published in 1984.⁴³ *Cranes Arise: Haiku Scenes,* my seventh book of haiku, was published in 1999.⁴⁴

NOTES

1. "Haiku Scenes," the introduction, has been revised and expanded from a shorter version of an essay published as "Haiku Traces" in *Native Liberty: Natural Reason and Cultural Survivance* by Gerald Vizenor (University of Nebraska Press, 2009), 257–76.

2. Matsuo Bashō, *The Narrow Road to the Deep North and Other Travel Sketches* (Baltimore: Penguin Books, 1966), 115, 116. Translated by Nobuyuki Yuasa.

3. Makoto Ueda, *The Path of Flowering Thorn: The Life and Poetry of Yosa Buson* (Stanford University Press, 1998), 1, 16.

4. R. H. Blyth, *A History of Haiku,* Volume One (Japan: Hokuseido, 1963), 7, 8, 40.

5. Blyth, *A History of Haiku,* Volume One, 1.

6. Kenneth Yasuda, *The Japanese Haiku* (Rutland, Vermont: Charles E. Tuttle Company, 1957), 24, 32.

7. Kobayashi Issa, *The Year of My Life* (Berkeley: University of California Press, 1960), 103, 104. *Oraga Haru,* translated by Nobuyuki Yuasa.

8. Stephen Addiss, *The Art of Haiku* (Boston: Shambhala, 2012), 260.

9. R. H. Blyth, *Haiku,* Volume IV, Autumn-Winter (Japan: Hokuseido, 1952), 230. Blyth wrote, "The poet or someone else has been playing the harp and at last leaves it on the tatami. Standing on the verandah, he gazes out at the rain which has fallen all day. It grows

darker and darker. Suddenly, the *koto* gives out a slight sound; a mouse must have scuttled across it."

10. R. H. Blyth, *Haiku: Eastern Culture,* Volume 1 (Japan: Hokuseido, 1949), 90.

11. Stephen Addiss, *The Art of Haiku,* 179.

12. Daisetz T. Suzuki, *Zen and Japanese Culture* (New York: Pantheon Books, Bollingen Series LXIV, 1959), 247.

13. Donald Keene, *Japanese Literature* (New York: Grove Press, 1955), 28, 29.

14. Frances Densmore, *Chippewa Music* (Minneapolis: Ross & Haines, 1973), 15.

15. Gerald Vizenor, *Summer in the Spring: Ojibwe Lyric Poems and Tribal Stories* (Minneapolis: Nodin Press, 1965), 23, 29. Frances Densmore, *Chippewa Music.*

16. Frances Densmore, *Chippewa Customs* (Minneapolis: Ross & Haines, 1970), 78, 79.

17. François Jullien, *The Propensity of Things* (New York: Zone Books, 1999), 11, 139, 140, 267.

18. John DeFrancis, *The Chinese Language* (Honolulu: University of Hawaii Press, 1984), 78, 92, 93.

19. Jullien, *The Propensity of Things,* 16, 143.

20. Kitaro Nishida, *An Inquiry into the Good* (New Haven: Yale University Press, 1990).

21. Blyth, *Haiku: Eastern Culture,* Volume 1, 343.

22. Donald Keene, *World Within Walls* (New York: Holt, Rinehart and Winston, 1976), 366. Keene asserted, "Issa is an unforgettable poet, but in the end he leaves us unsatisfied because he so rarely treated serious subjects. As a young man he must have known the horrors of the natural disasters that struck his part of the country, especially the eruption of Asama in 1783, but he never refers to them."

23. Gerald Vizenor, *Cranes Arise* (Minneapolis: Nodin Press, 1999).

24. Vizenor, *Summer in the Spring,* 25, 29.

25. Densmore, *Chippewa Music,* 129, 130.

26. Nishida, *An Inquiry into the Good.*

27. Daisetz T. Suzuki, *Zen and Japanese Culture* (New York: Pantheon Books, Bollingen Series, 1959), 225.

28. Nishida, *An Inquiry into the Good.*

29. Blyth, *Haiku,* Volume 1, 272.

30. Addiss, *The Art of Haiku,* 170, 171.

31. Makoto Ueda, *Bashō and His Interpreters* (Stanford University Press, 1991), 4.

32. Haruo Shirane, *Traces of Dreams: Landscape, Cultural Memory, and the Poetry of Bashō* (Stanford University Press, 1998), 157, 158.

33. Ueda, *Bashō and His Interpreters,* 372.

34. Gerald Vizenor, *Matsushima: Pine Islands* (Minneapolis: Nodin Press, 1984).

35. Haruo Shirane, *Traces of Dreams,* 223.

36. Issa, *The Year of My Life,* 139.

37. Robert Aitken, *A Zen Wave* (New York: Weatherhill, 1996), 14.

38. Gerald Vizenor, *Two Wings the Butterfly.* Privately printed in a limited edition of one hundred copies in the print shop at the Minnesota State Reformatory in Saint Cloud, Minnesota, 1962.

39. Gerald Vizenor, *Raising the Moon Vines* (Minneapolis: Callimachus Publishing Company, 1964). Reprinted by the Nodin Press, Minneapolis, in 1968, and 1999.

40. Gerald Vizenor, *Seventeen Chirps* (Minneapolis: Nodin Press, 1964, 1968).

41. Gerald Vizenor, Jerome Downes, *Slight Abrasions: A Dialogue in Haiku* (Minneapolis: Nodin Press, 1966).

42. Gerald Vizenor, *Empty Swings* (Minneapolis: Nodin Press, 1967).

43. Gerald Vizenor, *Matsushima: Pine Islands* (Minneapolis: Nodin Press, 1984).

44. Gerald Vizenor, *Cranes Arise* (Minneapolis: Nodin Press, 1999).

spring scenes

mounds of foam
beneath the waterfall
float silently

wooden bucket
frozen under a downspout
springs a leak

early morning
the old red waterwheel
starts to squeak

plum petals
tumble in the wet snow
blue feathers

windy morning
children under the lilacs
purple sway

apple trees
flower in the ides of march
snow petals

cocky wren
inspects a tiny bird house
scent of pine

easter sunday
children chase the chickens
moveable tease

windy night
acacia brightens a park bench
morning service

dreamy anhinga
wings spread in the sunlight
fish stories

march morning
meadowlarks on a fence post
change of music

catalpa flowers
scatter around a black cat
noisy birds

abandoned windmill
locked with rust over the well
creaks in a storm

warm rain
heartens the early tulips
dance of colors

thick ice
melts on a sandy beach
bright leaves

white catalpa
decorate the wet sidewalk
parade of doves

garden mice
scurry over the petals
gentle rain

broken ice
bears the veins of oak leaves
fade away

young raccoons
secure the old gardens
block by block

straw mounds
cover the new flower beds
shelter the mice

slivers of ice
chatter on the sandy shore
cautious birds

bright tulips
blue shadows on the snow
spring favors

warm rain
sway of concerts in the oaks
mockingbirds

calm lake
children dabble on the dock
cautious minnows

ice storm
new leaves shimmer overnight
words undone

maple beetles
dance outside the window
cat paws inside

gentle breeze
petals land in a rain barrel
sailboats

park bench
great blue trees in the snow
sundown shadows

dogwood petals
scattered in a gust of wind
faces in a pool

calico kittens
circle a saucer of milk
garden stones

paper boats
float with the street pirates
late for school

old woman
sneezes at the garden gate
lilacs in bloom

gentle rain
brightens the tangled shrubs
swarm of juncos

mighty birds
weave a nest with horse hair
caught on a fence

plastic kite
entangled in a cottonwood
rattles overnight

woodpeckers
sound of maple sugar taps
separate trees

double rainbow
rises out of the prairie
school recess

fish houses
gather one morning on shore
cracks in the ice

long underwear
surges on a windy clothesline
crows caw caw

moonlight
shadows grow in the garden
bright daffodils

windy boat dock
kites bounce over leech lake
birds of prey

city boy
rides a weary draft horse
twice to the barn

abandoned dock
gray posts and fishermen
some with hats

american crows
hopscotch over the garbage
customary court

march moon
bounces on the river ice
chunks afloat

late storm
tender faces in the snow
primroses

hilly path
stout man and a fat bulldog
out of breath

empty sleeves
moths arise from a scarecrow
twilight tease

earthworms
slither under the park swings
heavy rain

stone crossing
even the birds sing loudly
over the rapids

shiny crows
march on the railroad tracks
sprouted grain

black clouds
crows parade on the boat dock
crash of waves

rain clouds
float in a great convoy
birds in the reeds

tiger cat
leaps to catch a firefly
blinked twice

dogwood flowers
tremble in a thunderstorm
children at play

spring leaves
turn in a gentle rain
clumsy sparrow

whole moon
mongrels bark at the shadows
sounds in the marsh

gentle breeze
yellow cat waits on the porch
anemones spring

early morning
scruffy old man blew his nose
under the lilacs

lavender wisteria
brighten the cast iron gate
locked overnight

white butterflies
flutter over the bridal wreath
enchanted flight

city sparrows
chatter in the lilacs
rites of passage

gray morning
only the bright daffodils
change the weather

apple blossoms
disguise the muddy paths
heavy rain

bright dandelions
mark the grassy playground
natural crowns

may moon
blinks between the puffy clouds
faces alight

memorial day
raccoons on a garden tour
honor guards

cherry blossoms
ride on the black umbrellas
natural display

river shore
bright beams of morning light
break on the waves

crescent moon
adrift in the rain clouds
breaks away

blue herons
tease bashō in the shallows
spring waders

bright moon
boys stone the water tower
return chatter

ladybirds
parade on the birdfeeder
tricky choice

giant lilacs
swollen with overnight rain
solemn scent

golden eagles
circle over the horses
prairie sunset

morning glories
cover the broken fence
delayed repairs

scruffy sparrows
chatter outside the bakery
raisin scones

gentle rain
cat asleep on the front porch
doves in the eaves

birch leaves
bear the radiance of the sunset
favor of crows

spider webs
enhance the wooden fence
gentle rain

red tulips
wobble in the heavy rain
parade ground

mountain storm
faraway scent of lilacs
down river

maple leaves
frozen in the river ice
come ashore

cold wind
steady wheeze of the elm trees
robin nests

garden gate
glitters in the gentle rain
spider web

mighty crows
bounce over the great river
slippery stones

midnight moon
shimmers on lake namakan
sound of loons

summer scenes

sunday service
three mice escape the bellows
company of angels

early breakfast
under the morning glories
medals of honor

pony at the rail
bumps the children in a row
wet sleeves

dusty road
horses at the rusted gate
scent of mown hay

fat black cat
hidden in the summer sage
hummingbirds

noisy horseflies
circle the picnic bench
strawberry jelly

tiny blues
blossom in the granite seams
ancient bouquets

nara temple deer
graze with the hordes of tourists
chancy karma

bright hollyhocks
teeter in the rush of trains
flurry of faces

mosquitoes gather
overnight on the terrace
bloodline stories

wooden fence
secures a private garden
scent of jasmine

august sunrise
shimmers on the lawn chairs
drops of dew

daily newspapers
caught on the barbed wire fence
chatter overnight

ant mounds
flooded in a thunderstorm
restored by morning

morning glories
brighten the moist shadows
faces on a bench

balmy night
spider web near a street light
risky flight

chrysanthemums
lean over the garden mice
crown shadows

blue dragonflies
congregate in the cattails
hazy sunset

mosquitoes
swarm outside the tent
late night chorus

curious raccoon
swashes in a street puddle
moons ashore

overnight storm
green flies in the morning light
stray shadows

gypsy moths
flutter on the window screen
twilight music

downy catkins
caught in a spider web
waver overnight

honeysuckle
climbs a withered fruit tree
reach of memory

gusts of rain
trees turn away from the sea
beach stories

morning rain
robins chase the sidewalk worms
spring fare

spirited sparrows
chatter in the choir loft
six days a week

twilight mosquitoes
stories of ancestral blood
hatched in a culvert

summer heat
children gather with the flies
ice cream cart

wrens twitter
daily over the new house
painted pink

every footprint
erased by the gentle waves
tease of creation

flash of fireflies
bright stars between the leaves
nightly hearsay

clumsy horsefly
overturned on the sidewalk
buzzed rightly

tiny mosquitoes
gorge at a sunday picnic
crash in the weeds

red poppies
trace the motion of the sun
elders in the park

cold rain
old woman walks a mongrel
scent of cedar

party moths
danced last night in a lantern
sunrise stories

heavy hailstones
batter the tender corn stalks
radiant sunset

bright moon
bounces on lake namakan
wake of a canoe

great blue heron
steady steps in the shallows
waves of sunlight

morning sunlight
chases clouds on the meadow
crows alight

catalpa leaves
collected rain overnight
morning breeze

giant clouds
scatter in circles of waves
skipping stones

willow leaves
down overnight in a storm
laurels at dawn

green dragonflies
cross their wings in the cattails
sunrise ceremony

palace ravens
circle the best restaurant trash
imperial manners

tiny red spider
marches over the cascades
mountain map

temple butterfly
dithers on the white stones
scent of rain

tricky bullfrog
croaks a haiku in the marsh
skinny issa

china sunrise
tourists circle the statues
cicada fugues

box elder tree
children on a mighty bough
scent of oranges

tricky crows
spread their wings on a windmill
locked with rust

fat green flies
square dance across the grapefruit
honor your partner

windy morning
robins in the chokecherry tree
tipsy flight

black butterflies
dance on the chrysanthemums
double time

trumpet vines
decorate the ancient oak
natural union

clothes line
children run between the sheets
shadow encore

persistent moths
flutter in the porch lanterns
port in a storm

misty moon
shimmers on the sidewalk
snail traces

morning mist
cardinals ride in the white pine
rowers on the river

early breakfast
black flies first to the table
rural habits

marsh marigolds
tremble in the hard rain
faces on a bus

gray gardener
raises a red umbrella
over the roses

whole moons
float with the river faces
beneath the bridge

old school bell
sounds once or twice a summer
hailstones

bold nasturtiums
dress the barbed wire fences
down to the sea

broken windmill
meadowlarks perch on the blades
prairie music

old gray stump
remembers the past today
raising the moon vines

rusted nails
on the morning glory fence
wet with dew

cattle birds
ride the cows in the pasture
yellow school bus

twilight at clear lake
old friends row in the distance
herons in the reeds

white butterflies
flutter around the children
picking flowers

hummingbirds
court the african lilies
day after day

leech lake storm
two plovers run with the waves
dance partners

shaggy mare
once pranced in summer parades
leans at the gate

early light
redwing blackbirds in the reeds
squeak of oars

crescent moon
fireflies in the moist grass
hands alight

trumpet vines
reach over the wooden fence
bright bouquet

blue bell flowers
wobble on a windy day
butterflies

mountain stream
aspen leaves caught in the foam
sail out to sea

purple grackles
screech on the telephone wires
sunday picnic

autumn scenes

calm in the storm
master bashō soaks his feet
water striders

haughty ravens
roost in the bare cottonwoods
oversee the river

maple leaves
bright ceremonial mounds
smolder overnight

whole moon
slowly moves through the window
traces in a book

red maple leaves
set sail with the river boats
ports of call

harvest moon
parades over the garden
one stalk at a time

willow leaves
brighter in the autumn moon
float away

noisy ravens
gather one early morning
crack of pecans

october moon
shivers in a rain barrel
curious raccoon

blue ravens
glimmer in the cottonwoods
twilight hues

flights of starlings
curve and shimmer wing to wing
sunset sway

cold wind
leaves scatter across the bandstand
last dance

redwing blackbirds
bounce on the reeds in the slough
curtain calls

gray squirrel
hunkers at the windowsill
early breakfast

broken fence
horses browse in the orchard
crack of apples

first frost
moths flutter at the windows
billets-doux

cedar cones
tumble over the river stones
wash ashore

autumn wind
garage doors open and close
wings of a moth

late night
new moon on a country road
whistlestops in the dark

spider web
woven over the harness
caught a weary fly

autumn leaves
mountains erupt with children
late for school

sunday morning
two hearts entwined on the bridge
crossed out overnight

chilly night
crickets chirp in a down spout
last words

cedar waxwings
silent in the red sumac
turn with the leaves

overnight snow
brightens the summer paths
courts the crows

november moon
creeps over the bare boughs
lightens the leaves

cold mist
glistens on the dark shoreline
river ghosts

heavy frost
horses on the gray meadow
plumes of breath

oak leaves
cover a broken park bench
autumn disguise

windy schoolyard
mongrels gather at the gate
speedy lesson

weary crickets
rehearse night after night
culvert chorus

spider web
billows on a bare bough
empty

old man
pitches pennies in a pond
leaves afloat

crispy leaves
driven by a prairie wind
float on the river

charcoal bags
stored in the summer shed
smell of urine

gusts of wind
pushed the leaves down a tin roof
lonely night

gray juncos
gather in the red maples
gorgeous ruins

bright pansies
save face in the first light snow
close overnight

box elder bough
leans over to the gazebo
squeaks in the wind

steady breeze
bends the whiskers of the cat
asleep on the stoop

bright moon
country man salutes his shirt
weathered scarecrow

autumn night
leaves and family secrets
take flight

timothy grass
waves beside the windy road
sway of memory

morning frost
remains in the hoary boughs
scent of cedar

early october
white moths in the paper birch
stack of firewood

lake itasca
red squirrels bark in the pine
twilight stories

autumn sunset
great blue herons stand alone
change of colors

wet leaves
slither over the window panes
blurry trees

empty swings
move slowly in the wind
cold shadows

picnic bench
sparrows gather for the crumbs
light snow

cedar waxwings
overnight near the bower
depart at dawn

cold morning
sound of a downy woodpecker
breaks the silence

sunset beams
shimmer in the great red pine
shadow dance

birch leaves
brighten the new gravestones
cold october

[88]

sundogs
break over the meadow
fugitive light

empty wren house
hanging in a fruit tree
squeaks overnight

windy morning
heavy clouds over leech lake
crows on the dock

red sumac
bright in the autumn sunset
evening grosbeak

cold rain
brightens the black metal gate
morning mail

windy shoreline
blackbirds rebound in the cattails
fur trade routes

brown ants
parade around the rain pools
leaves afloat

field mouse
scurries in a ceiling light
risky nest

red squirrels
capture the short maple tree
almost bare

rain and sleet
children hunched at the bus stop
yellow boots

bold crows
march over the park benches
first light snow

loyal mongrels
lead the children to school
early lessons

autumn ghosts
hover in the norway pine
vanish at dawn

beach crows
wait for the old fisherman
remains of the catch

black flies
wait for the warm sunrise
last autumn flights

river stones
sparkle under the thin ice
ancient bridge

lily pads
wave in an icy wind
frozen overnight

cold rain
field mice rattle the dishes
buson's koto

texas cotton
caught in the roadside stubble
december flowers

first snow
squirrels tied the trees together
double bows

mountain snow
warblers search for apricots
no regrets

scruffy bird nests
covered overnight with snow
dream songs

tiny tracks
circle the icy boulders
trickle of water

wispy clouds
display the sunset hues
winter light

narrow path
curves with the slant of snow
chimney smoke

rosy sunset
chases a child in the snow
giant shadows

light snow
bird tracks under a pine tree
white cat

city sparrows
chatter under the eaves
strong wind

school children
captains of the window ice
sail on the sunlight

white spruce
crows loosen the first snow
sunrise spectacle

white birch
moody shadows in the snow
grave houses

red squirrel
barks on bare birch bough
timber wolves

wet snow
covers one side of the trees
face the wind

thin clouds
stretch across the night sky
tease the moon

snow caves
reach over the river bank
melt away

northern lights
great circles on the ice
moonlight skaters

willow leaves
frozen in the clear ice
mock the season

gray sparrows
gather around the brown crusts
frozen overnight

wooden ladder
crowned overnight with wet snow
stands alone

final leaves
tumble with the children
heavy snow

blue jays
drink from the watery names
warm gravestones

sudden storm
geraniums in the window
wait to be turned

catalpa pods
rattle in the bitter wind
snowbound

mongrels
circle the very same trees
traces in the snow

red sumac
bounce in the gusts of snow
lost leaves

woman in the park
feeds the moody pigeons
lends an ear

tick of snow
crickets chirp in a flower pot
nightly aria

daily newspapers
stacked under the window
elevates the cat

stubborn cattails
burst in a cold gust of wind
lost mittens

gray squirrels
bounce between the bare trees
mounds of snow

garden chairs
plushy cushions overnight
heavy snow

black cats
hiss each other in the snow
no place to hide

park bench
covered with mounds of snow
giants for a day

shoreline pine
shaped by the steady wind
lean away

shiny ravens
bounce in the heavy snow
shadow dance

break in the ice
sun shimmers on the water
geese alight

ornamental tree
crouches under the window
snowy boughs

white birch
stacked near the summer house
mouse parade

brown ants
three stories high in a urinal
delay the flush

plastic flowers
decorate the old gravestones
familiar names

giant icicles
crash outside the window
early equinox

cherry tree
shadows entwined in the snow
crows arrive

pinyons
shoulder mounds of wet snow
desert favors

cold night
skaters on a moonlit lake
break the silence

mountain creek
trickles around the stones
sounds of spring

gray juncos
return for spring rehearsals
early concert

snowflakes
alight in a cup of tea
temple stories

cold morning
puffy birds at the windows
close to home

winter rain
glazes the red sumac
shiny browse

bright moon
shimmers in the rose window
seams icey

family diner
outlasts the railroad station
scent of cinnamon

timber wolves
raise their voices overnight
trickster stories

gray squirrel
chatters over the birdfeeder
out of reach

old man
preens at the slushy bus stop
shiny black boots

river beaver
break the ice overnight
birch afloat

ocean storm
ravens ride the monterey pine
out of breath

chunks of snow
tumble through the cedar boughs
change of season

overnight thaw
stench of buried dog shit
close to home

flower garden
buried in heavy snow
sway of memory

red squirrel
chatters on a broken bough
snow crowns

lake itasca
source of the great river
buried in snow

white earth
memories of the last storm
scent of cedar

first cardinals
bounce in the gray withered trees
trace of daffodils

waves of snow
decorate a wooden fence
squirrel routes

snow crusts
final traces of winter
praise the totems

raucous crows
circle the moored ice houses
nightly stories

white tail deer
reach higher for the browse
crusted snow

grand marais
old fur traders tease the fire
survivance stories

snowy mountain
green traces of aspen leaves
spring overnight

winter ends
one morning in a warm rain
crocus count

about the author

Gerald Vizenor is a prolific writer and literary critic, and a citizen of the White Earth Nation of the Anishinaabeg in Minnesota. He is Professor Emeritus of American Studies at the University of California, Berkeley. Vizenor is the author of several novels, books of poetry, and critical studies of Native American culture, identity, politics, and literature.